CAMBRIDGE GEOGRAPHY PROJECT

PROBLEM SOLVING WITH MAPS

Stuart Marson

Deputy Head, Eirias High School, Colwyn Bay

David Lambert

Series Editor

CAMBRIDGE
UNIVERSITY PRESS

Preface

Published by the Press Syndicate of the University of Cambridge
The Pitt Building, Trumpington Street, Cambridge CB2 1RP
40 West 20th Street, New York, NY 10011-4211, USA
10 Stamford Road, Oakleigh, Melbourne 3166, Australia

© Cambridge University Press 1992

First published 1992

Printed in Hong Kong by Wing King Tong Company Ltd

A catalogue record for this book is available from the British Library.

ISBN 0 521 42843 2

Designed and produced by The Pen and Ink Book Company Ltd, Huntingdon, Cambridgeshire

Illustrated by Pen and Ink, Rodney Sutton and John York

Cover artwork by Jane Smith

Acknowledgements
Extracts from Ordnance Survey maps are reproduced with the permission of the Controller of Her Majesty's Stationery Office © Crown Copyright: p.5 from 1986 1:25 000 sheet SP43/53; from the 1:50 000 series – p.7 1990 sheet 162, p.19 1990 sheet 151, p.21 1989 sheet 115, p.29 1987 sheet 132, p.35 1991 sheet 152, pp.39 and 48 1987 sheet 203. Other items: p.11 Brian J. Green; p.12 National Maritime Museum; Zefa: p.15 a and d, p.24, p.42; J. Allan Cash: p.15 b and c, p.41; p.17 © Bartholemew. Reproduced by kind permission; p.20 Christian Bonington; p.25 National Remote Sensing Centre Ltd; p.31 Retna Pictures Ltd – Gary Gershoff; p.32 Katherine James; p.43 Welsh Orienteering Association; p.46 Colwyn Borough Council.

This book is about cartography, the study of maps. We use maps in our everyday lives to answer questions, to make decisions and to solve problems:

▷ Which is the best route to the coast?

▷ Where is the nearest car park to the shops?

▷ Where are they planning to build the bypass?

▷ Will we be able to see the new factory chimney from our house?

This book presents a series of problems that can only be solved by using maps. In this way, the skills of map use can be learnt and developed. As with problem solving in general, the approach lends itself to individual or group work.

Teachers should bear in mind that the book covers much of the National Curriculum Key Stage 3 Attainment Target 1 (Geographical Skills). The structure and content of the book allow it to be used alongside the core books of the Cambridge Geography Project.

As with many areas of geography, pupils will encounter new, specialised words that relate to mapwork. These are presented in *italics* in the text, to help pupils build up a mapwork vocabulary.

Contents

Mental maps
Sketch maps

How many different maps do you have at home? You may have some road maps or a street map of the area where you live. You may also have some *Ordnance Survey* maps. The Ordnance Survey is the main organisation that makes maps in Britain.

There is another place where maps are kept: in your mind. You will have stored, in your mind, mental maps of the area where you live and of places that you visit from time to time – the 'jigsaw pieces' of the world around you.

Sketched from memory, a mental map of your neighbourhood will look something like this, showing the places you know best.

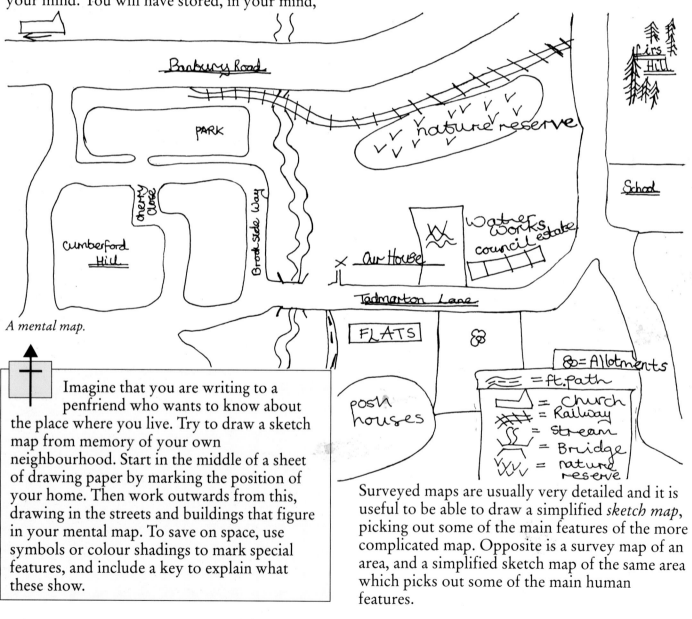

A mental map.

Imagine that you are writing to a penfriend who wants to know about the place where you live. Try to draw a sketch map from memory of your own neighbourhood. Start in the middle of a sheet of drawing paper by marking the position of your home. Then work outwards from this, drawing in the streets and buildings that figure in your mental map. To save on space, use symbols or colour shadings to mark special features, and include a key to explain what these show.

Surveyed maps are usually very detailed and it is useful to be able to draw a simplified *sketch map*, picking out some of the main features of the more complicated map. Opposite is a survey map of an area, and a simplified sketch map of the same area which picks out some of the main human features.

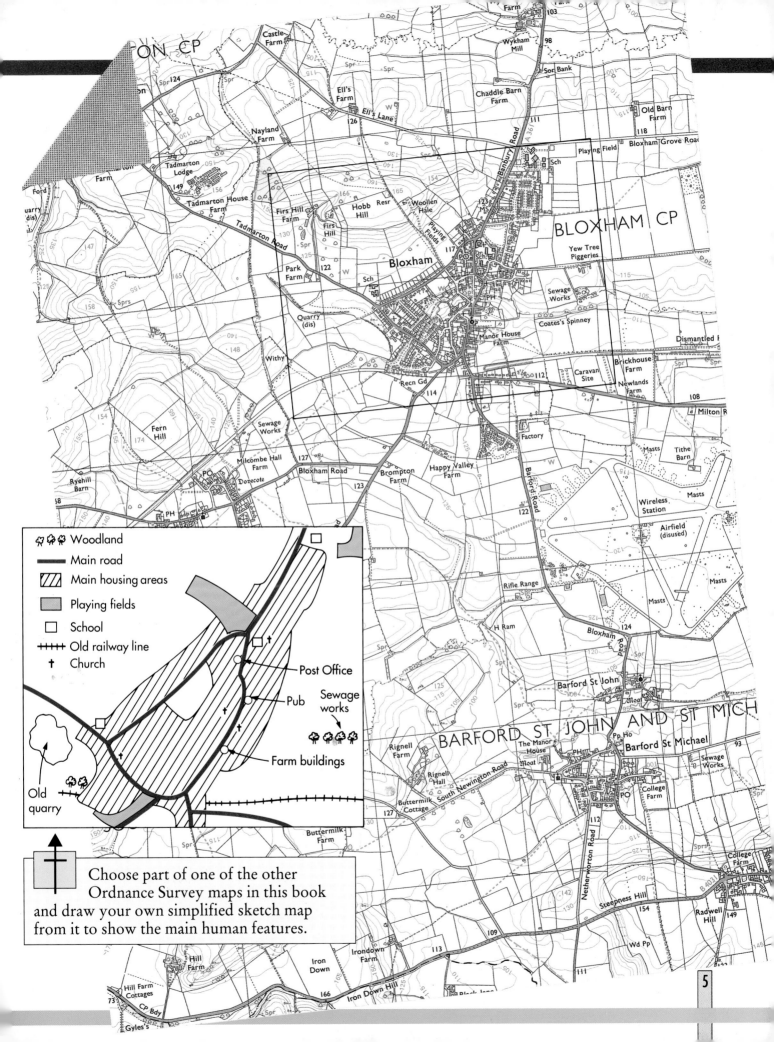

Legend (sketch map key):

- 🌳🌳🌳 Woodland
- ▬▬ Main road
- ▨ Main housing areas
- ▨ Playing fields
- ☐ School
- ┼┼┼┼ Old railway line
- ✝ Church

Post Office

Pub

Sewage works

🌳🌳🌳🌳

Farm buildings

Old quarry

Choose part of one of the other Ordnance Survey maps in this book and draw your own simplified sketch map from it to show the main human features.

Map labels:

ON CP · Castle Farm · Farm · 103 · Wykham Mill · 98 · Sor Bank · 124 · Spr · Ell's Farm · Ell's Lane · Chaddle Barn Farm · 111 · 110 · 115 · Old Barn Farm · 118 · 26 · Nayland Farm · W · A 361 · Banbury Road · 130 · Tadmarton Lodge · 149 · 156 · Tadmarton House Farm · Firs Hill Farm · Hobb Hill · Resr · Woollen Hale · Playing Field · Bloxham Grove Road · Sch · 154 · 166 · 165 · Playing Fields · 123 · MS · BLOXHAM CP · Tadmarton Road · 130 · Firs Hill · Spr · 125 · 122 · Park Farm · W · Sch · 117 · Bloxham · PO · Sch · Yew Tree Piggeries · 115 · 105 · 147 · 165 · Quarry (dis) · Sch · PH · Sewage Works · Coates's Spinney · Dismantled · 158 · Withy · Manor House Farm · 112 · Brickhouse Farm · Caravan Site · Newlands Farm · 108 · 148 · 140 · Recn Gd · 114 · Milton R · 154 · 174 · Fern Hill · 170 · 155 · 150 · Sewage Works · Factory · Masts · Tithe Barn · Masts · Ryehill Barn · Milcombe Hall Farm · 127 · PO · Dovecote · Bloxham Road · Brompton Farm · 123 · Happy Valley Farm · 125 · Barford Road · 122 · Wireless Station · Masts · 58 · PH · Airfield (disused) · 120 · Rifle Range · Masts · Masts · H Ram · Bloxham Road · 124 · Buttermilk Farm · 120 · Spr · Spr · 125 · 115 · 100 · Spr · Barford St John · Moat · 106 · BARFORD ST JOHN AND ST MICH · Rignell Farm · The Manor House · Moat · Barford St Michael · 93 · Rignell Hall · Pp Ho · PH · Sewage Works · Buttermilk Cottage · South Newington Road · Netherworton Road · PO · College Farm · 112 · 127 · 30 · Buttermilk Farm · Spr · 115 · 142 · 125 · 160 · Steepness Hill · 154 · College Farm · Radwell Hill · 149 · 109 · 113 · Ironic Down Farm · Iron Down · 111 · Wd Pp · Hill Farm · 150 · 166 · Iron Down Hill · Black Lane · Hill Farm Cottages · 73 · CP Bdy · Gyles's · **5**

Decoding messages
Scale and reference

Surveyed maps are different from sketch maps because they are *drawn to scale*. The scale of an Ordnance Survey map is usually shown by a ratio that appears on the map cover. This shows how much the real world is scaled down on the map. 1 : 50 000 and 1 : 25 000 are common scales for Ordnance Survey maps. The figure means that one unit of measurement on the ground is shown at 1/50 000th, or 1/25 000th, scale on the map.

Surveyed maps are also criss-crossed by grid lines. The vertical lines are called *eastings* and the horizontal lines are called *northings*. Any point on a map with grid lines showing eastings and northings can be described by a *4-figure grid reference*. Remember that eastings are followed by northings in a grid reference.

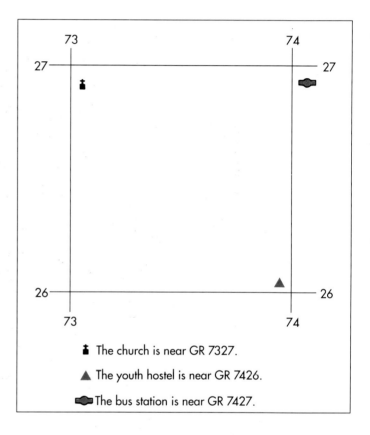

🪦 The church is near GR 7327.

▲ The youth hostel is near GR 7426.

🚌 The bus station is near GR 7427.

You are an officer with MI5, the British Secret Service. Recently, a coded message has been intercepted by MI5, who believe that it was sent by an enemy spy. As you are an expert in decoding, you have been asked to try to make sense of the message. Can you crack the code?

It is thought that the spy lives in the map area shown opposite. The spy is known to have used 4-figure grid references in the past to make up coded messages – you will need to look for a name or height number on the map near to each grid reference.

The coded message reads as above:

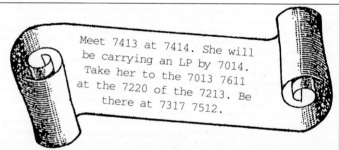

Meet 7413 at 7414. She will be carrying an LP by 7014. Take her to the 7013 7611 at the 7220 of the 7213. Be there at 7317 7512.

Try to make up your own coded message like the one above. You could also use map symbols and shadings in place of letters of the alphabet to make up the name of a country. Then swap with someone in your class to see how good you are at code cracking.

Bending scale
Topological maps

Maps are usually drawn to scale according to distance. For example, on a 1 : 50000 Ordnance Survey map, 2 centimetres are equal to 1 kilometre on the ground.

However, sometimes maps are not drawn according to a distance scale. Look at the two maps of South America below. The first map shows the South American countries drawn to a distance scale. However, the map on the right looks very different. This is because Gross National Product has been chosen for the scale for the map. When drawn using this scale, the different levels of development of the countries in South America stand out clearly. On the left-hand map, Brazil stands out as being the largest country in South America. However, as the second map shows, it is by no means the richest.

Maps drawn to a scale other than a distance scale are called *topological maps*.

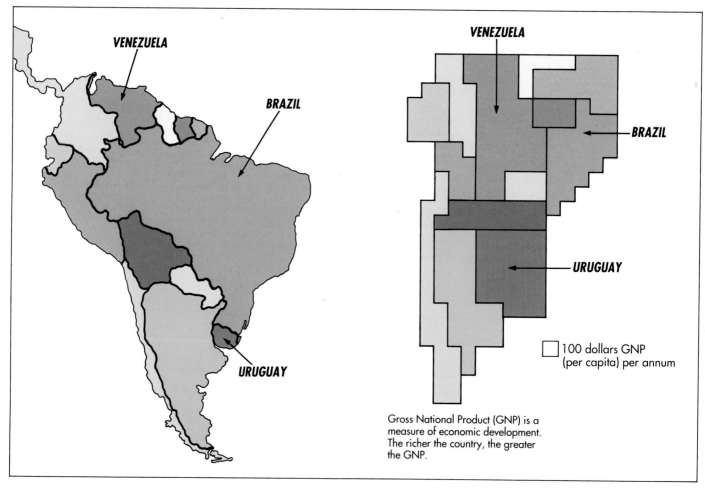

100 dollars GNP (per capita) per annum

Gross National Product (GNP) is a measure of economic development. The richer the country, the greater the GNP.

South America.
Left: drawn to a distance scale. Right: drawn to a topological scale.

The Governor of the state of New South Wales in Australia has just received the following figures showing the number of foreign tourists visiting each Australian state during the peak summer month of January.

New South Wales	210,000
Western Australia	175,000
Queensland	142,000
Victoria	95,000
South Australia	65,000
Northern Territory	55,000
Tasmania	44,000

He asks you, as his advertising executive, to produce a poster which will show the success of New South Wales in attracting tourists. He advises you that the poster must include a topological map of Australia based on the figures he has received.

To create the topological map, look carefully at the shape of Australia and its states in the map below. You will need to use a squared overlay or graph paper to produce your topological map. Your first task is to choose a value for each square. Be thoughtful in doing this – otherwise your map may be too big or too small.

To help you to decide on illustrations for your poster, do some research into the tourist attractions of New South Wales.

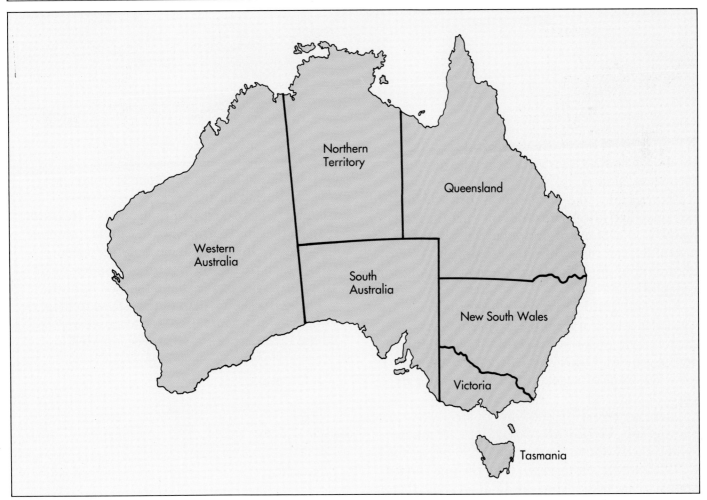

Australia drawn to a distance scale.

A bird's eye view
Air photographs

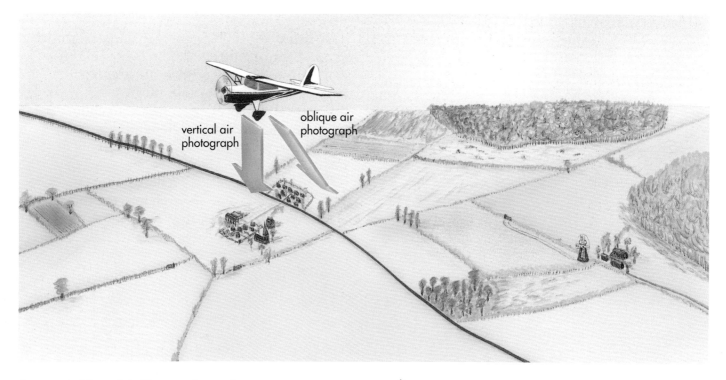

vertical air photograph

oblique air photograph

A map is like a bird's eye view of an area. It shows the land as if you were flying over it in an aeroplane.

Photographs taken from the air provide lots of extra detailed information about what the land below is like. Some of this detail is more than a map alone can show. For this reason, air photographs are very useful when used alongside a map of an area.

Air photographs have some important specialist uses. For example, archaeologists use them to help pick out the traces of old buildings on the ground. Other specialists can use them to see what crops or vegetation are growing in an area.

There are two different types of air photograph. *Vertical air photographs* are taken from directly above the ground (at 90 degrees to it). *Oblique air photographs* (like the one shown opposite) are taken from the air at an angle that is less than 90 degrees to the ground below.

Greybeard, the high-tech pirate, has buried his treasure on an isolated island. He has asked you to produce a treasure map so that his treasure hoard can be found in the future. However, he has only indicated where each part of his treasure is hidden on an air photograph of the island (shown opposite).

Using the sketch map of the island to help you, draw a treasure map, showing clearly where each part of the treasure is hidden.

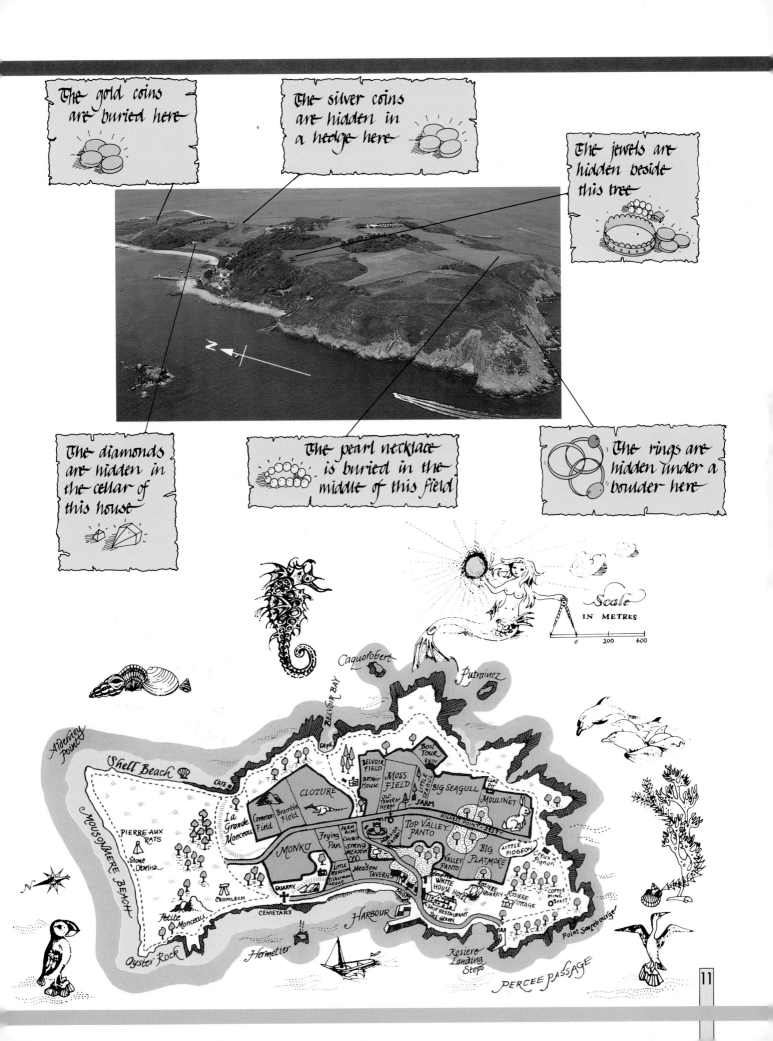

The gold coins are buried here

The silver coins are hidden in a hedge here

The jewels are hidden beside this tree

The diamonds are hidden in the cellar of this house

The pearl necklace is buried in the middle of this field

The rings are hidden under a boulder here

Scale
IN METRES
0   200   400

Caquorobert

Putrainez

Belvoir Bay

Alderney Point

Shell Beach

Café

Belvoir Field

Belvoir House

Bon Tour Ruin

Moss Field

Little Seagull

Big Seagull

Cloture

Old Tower or Herm

Moulinet

La Grande Monceau

Common Field

Bramble Field

Farm Bldg

Clay Pit

Pierre aux Rats

Stone Obelisk

Monku

Frying Pan

Church

Spring Meadow

Top Valley Panto

Highest Point

Big Platmore

Little Pidgeon

Creux à Pignon

Little Meadow

Directors Area

Meadow Tavern

Valley Panto

Rosiere Quarry

Rosiere Cottage

Copper Mine Shaft

Quarry

Cromlech

Shop

White House Hotel

The Green

Petite Monceau

Cemetary

Harbour

Ship Restaurant

Mousonniere Beach

Oyster Rock

Hermetier

Rosiere Landing Steps

Point Sampesbourge

PERCEE PASSAGE

A world view
Map projections

It is the year 1607 and you are John, the eldest son of Willem Blaeu, the renowned map maker. Your family has for some time been trying to perfect a map of the world. The globe shown on this page is one of the best 'maps' of the world they have to refer to. But how can a globe be turned satisfactorily into a map on a flat piece of paper? (Cartographers call the means of doing this a *map projection*.) Can you solve the problem?

You will need something globe-shaped to work with. This could be a fruit that can be peeled, like an orange or a grapefruit, or an old plastic ball will do, if you don't mind cutting it up!

You will also need a globe to look at so that you can see the positions of the continents. Find a way of drawing the outline of each of the continents onto your globe-shaped object. Viewed from four different directions, your 'globe' should look something like the diagrams opposite.

Then use a knife to remove the peel of your fruit, or scissors to cut up your ball. Think very carefully before you do this so that you work out the best way of doing it. When your 'globe' is laid flat, there will be some gaps between the bits of peel or ball.

Finally, transfer your 'globe' to paper by carefully drawing around the edge of the peel or ball and drawing in the position of each continent. This is your completed map projection.

A world globe made in 1551 by Gerard Mercator.

The problem you have been working on was also tackled by Gerard Mercator at about the same time as Blaeu. You should be able to find a Mercator projection of the world in an atlas. How is it similar to and different from your projection?

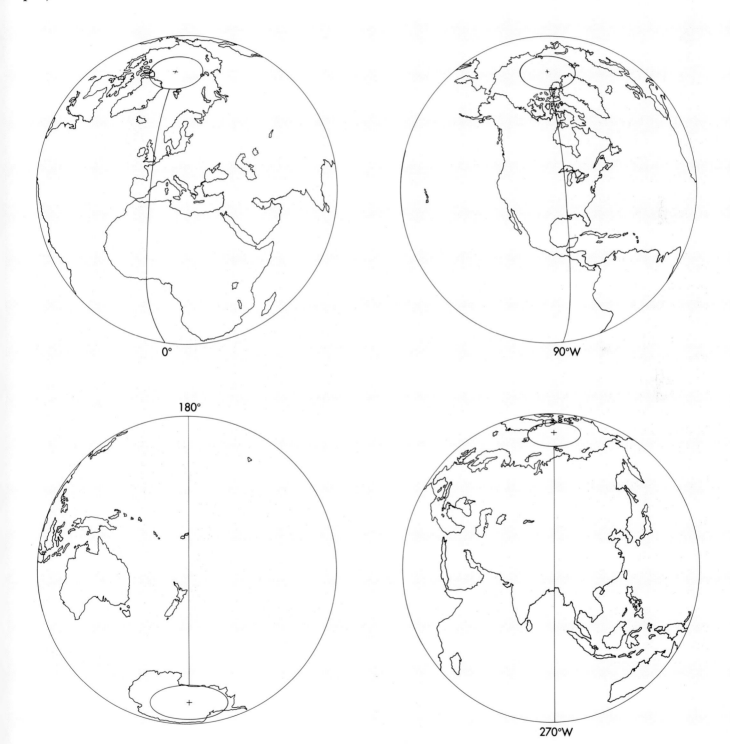

Around the world
Using an atlas

In the book *Around the World in 80 Days* written by Jules Verne, Phileas Fogg sets off in an attempt to travel around the world in 80 days.

Although the story is only make-believe, many people have attempted to make this journey.

Phileas Fogg and his manservant, Passepartout, descended, the street-door was double-locked, and at the end of Saville Row they took a cab and drove rapidly to Charing Cross. The cab stopped before the railway station at twenty minutes past eight. Passepartout jumped off the box and followed his master into the station.

Two first-class tickets for Paris having been speedily purchased, Mr Fogg was crossing the station to the train when he perceived his five friends of the Reform Club.

'Well gentlemen,' said he, 'I'm off, you see; and if you will examine my passport when I get back, you will be able to judge whether I have accomplished the journey agreed upon.'

'Oh, that would be quite unnecessary, Mr Fogg,' said Ralph politely. 'We will trust your word, as a gentleman of honour.'

'You do not forget when you are due in London again?' asked Stuart.

'In eighty days; on Saturday, the 21st of December, 1872, at a quarter before nine p.m. Goodbye, gentlemen.'

Phileas Fogg and his servant seated themselves in a first-class carriage at twenty minutes before nine; five minutes later the whistle screamed, and the train slowly glided out of the station.

30

Can *you* plan a trip to take you around the world in 80 days? Like Phileas Fogg, you must start from the centre of London and you must visit the following places on your journey:

Dover ○
○ Venice
Hong Kong ○
Plymouth (UK) ○
○ Calais
○ Suez
○ Calcutta
Bombay ○
○ San Francisco
Alexandria ○
○ Halifax (Canada)

Hong Kong.

Venice.

Suez Canal.

You can travel by boat, train or road transport, but you cannot use air transport. Use an atlas to locate places visited along your route, and work out the distances between the places.

You can cover 30 kilometres per hour by boat and 80 kilometres per hour by train or road transport. You will need to allow extra time at each place where you need to change from one form of transport to another – add on 12 hours at each point where this happens.

Present your plan for attempting to travel around the world in 80 days in the form of a table like the one below. For each section of the journey, show the distance covered, form of travel and time taken. At the foot of the table, add up the total journey time.

Did you make it around the world within 80 days?

From	To	Form of transport	Time taken

Golden Gate Bridge, San Francisco.

Linear maps
Route description

Some of our mental maps store information about the routes that we follow, for example from home to a relative's house some distance away.

Drawn as sketch maps, these come out as linear maps. A *linear map* shows a route and the places, buildings or landmarks (in order) that are passed along the way.

> Draw a simple linear map of a route that you often follow. It could be your journey to school, the route to a friend's house, or the route to the shops in your nearest town or village centre.

Linear maps often appear in road atlases to show main routes that people may want to follow.

> You are spending your holiday in the resort of Swanage, and your great-aunt Felicity, who lives in Bath, sends you this postcard:

Travelling northwards along the M1 from St Albans to Milton Keynes

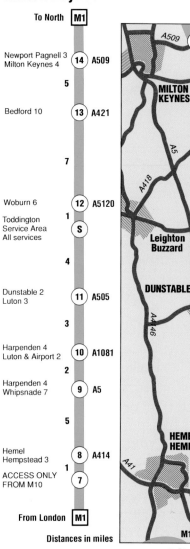

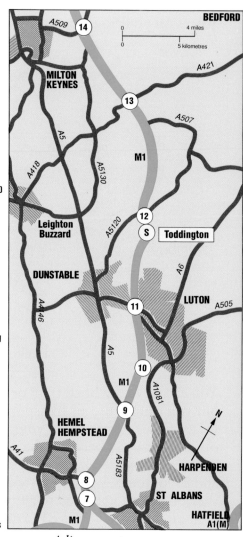

A linear route map: St Albans to Milton Keynes.

Dear All,

I will drive down to visit you in Swanage on Friday. I plan to leave home at 3 p.m. Could you please send me directions for the best route I can take? Remember, I'm a bit nervous about driving and want to avoid going through busy towns and cities as far as possible. I hope to hear from you soon.

Love,
Great-aunt Felicity

J & L Reader

Bay View Guest House

Swanage

Dorset BH19 1ZZ

You phone the AA to check for roadworks and other likely hold-ups in the area and are told of the following:

- Single file traffic / temporary lights on the A350 at East Knoyle and Fontmell Magna (both near the town of Shaftesbury)

- Heavy traffic expected at Corfe Castle (historic pageant) and Warminster (carnival parade)

Draw a linear map to send to great-aunt Felicity. Colour the sections of the route according to road type:

    A roads: *red*
    B roads: *brown*
    minor roads: *yellow*.

Label the places she will pass through along the route (in the correct order).

Extract from a road atlas map.

The chocolate delivery
Following a route on a map

You have a friend who is passionately fond of milk chocolates. However, delivering them is something of a problem, and you employ a special messenger to do it. The messenger later provides you with a description of his route (below). Can you follow his description on the map opposite? You will find a ruler and a protractor useful. You will need to look at the Ordnance Survey map symbols on page 48.

I parachuted out at 2,000 metres, and the moonlight revealed an electricity transmission line appearing rapidly below. I veered off and landed beside a farm building. Nearby was a minor road, which I crossed as dawn broke. I made my way along a footpath to a triangulation point on a nearby small hill. I took my bearings and decided to walk for 2.75 kilometres along bearing 142.

At the wood, I followed a small stream until I reached the canal. Borrowing a rowing boat that was moored nearby, I made my way along the canal to the nearest lock. I needed to check the time, so I went directly to the nearest public telephone box.

From there, I followed a footpath to the nearest church and on the top of the tower I assembled my portable hang-glider. I took off and flew for 4 kilometres along bearing 090. I eventually landed beside a radio mast.

Quickly I ran down to the minor road and headed off in a northerly direction. After the crossroads, I followed the county boundary until I reached a point exactly halfway between two disused windmills. I walked up the hill to the windpump and then followed the footpath as far as the church tower. I ran through the park and along the main road to a milepost near a hamlet.

In the Post Office window was a message: 'Follow the gated road to the T-junction where a taxi will be waiting.' The taxi hurried me 3 kilometres to the south. Passing a church tower in a village to my left, we turned off left and then left again, up a steep hill. By the pub, I left the taxi and walked along a bearing of 125 degrees for 2.8 kilometres. At a small building, I followed a new bearing of 325 degrees for 1.3 kilometres. At last, with the box of chocolates clutched in my hand, I arrived at my destination.

▶ Where was the box of chocolates delivered?

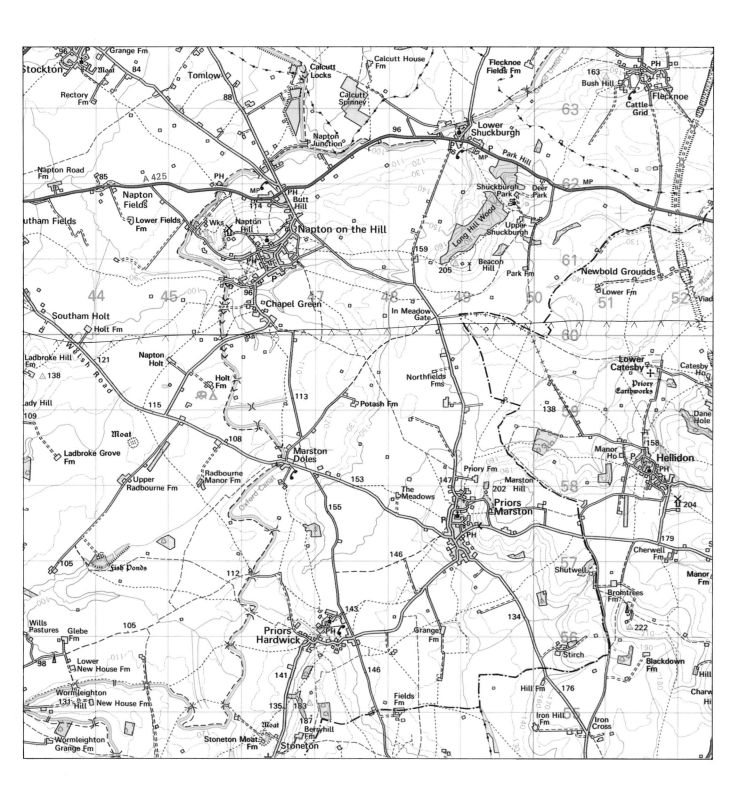

A mountain to climb
Looking at relief

In geography, the shape of the land surface is called *relief*. On maps, *contour lines* are drawn to show the relief features. These are brown *isopleths* (see pages 32–33) which join up places that are at the same height above sea level.

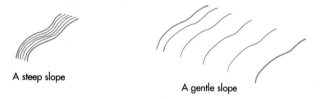

A steep slope

A gentle slope

Where the contour lines are drawn close together, the land is steep. Where the contours are widely spaced, the land slopes gently. If no contours appear on a map area, this means that the land is flat. Sometimes the land is so steep that the contour lines can't all be drawn in on the map. In these cases, *hachure lines* are drawn on the map to show the steepness of the slope. (An example can be seen near GR 6854 on the map extract opposite.)

Mount Everest (the highest mountain in the world) remained unclimbed until 1953, when an expedition led by Sir John Hunt was successful, with Sherpa Tensing and Sir Edmund Hillary reaching the summit. Their success was based on the careful selection of a route that would take them over the least difficult relief.

The route that they selected is shown on the diagram below. It climbed up a glacier-filled valley into a *cwm* (a high mountain hollow). They then climbed up to a high mountain pass (called a *col*). The final ascent to the summit was up a knife-edged ridge (called an *arête*).

Mount Everest and the route of the 1953 expedition.

The Striders' Walking Club have asked you to lead a party on a trek to the summit of Carnedd Moel Siabod (a mountain summit in Wales). Most of the club members are new to mountain walking, so you need to select a route that is fairly easy-going and safe. They will be dropped off by coach at the car park near GR 6654.

Using tracing paper or a photocopy of the map, work out the best route for the walk. Then write a short letter to the Striders' Walking Club, describing the route you have chosen and the relief it will cover.

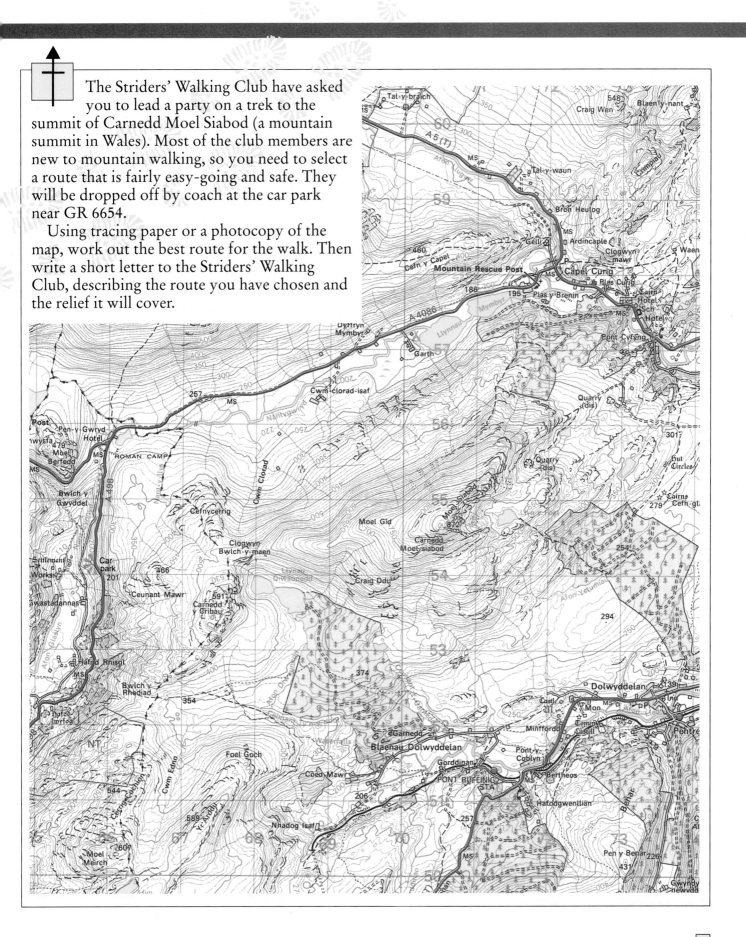

Planning a golf course
Looking at relief

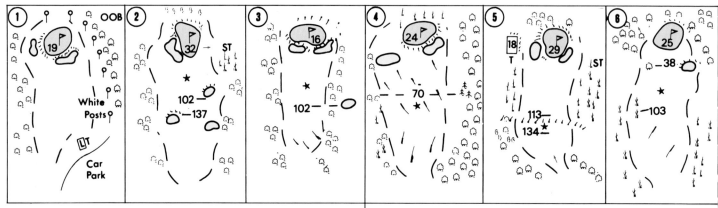

Maps from part of a golf course score card.

Key to diagrams

All fairway yards to centre of greens	← To next tee
All distances in yards	ST Staked trees
★ Indicates 200 yds from back of men's tee	⚲ White posts

Greenford Park is the former country estate of Lord and Lady Parr. It is situated in the Green Belt outside a large British city. It has recently been sold to Primeshare PLC, a company that intends to develop it as an 18-hole golf course. The company asks you to prepare a plan for the layout of the golf course. The guidelines for you to work to are as follows:

1 The course should be between 4 km and 5 km in length.

2 The length of individual holes will vary. The 7 longest holes will each be approximately 550 metres long and there will be 5 short holes, each approximately 200 metres in length.

3 The natural features of the park (hills, viewpoints, lakes, streams, etc.) should be used to make an interesting and challenging course.

4 The park contains some obstacles that you will need to avoid in your plan. Safety is also an important consideration.

5 Greenford House will be the clubhouse, and the course should start and finish near it.

6 A bad-weather shelter will be needed halfway around the course.

Prepare your plan by tracing the map of Greenford Park. On your plan, mark the numbered tees and holes clearly, and lines showing the fairways connecting them. The first tee (T_1) and the first hole (H_1) are already shown on the map.

When your plan is finished, write a short article for *Golfer's World* magazine, describing and explaining your course layout.

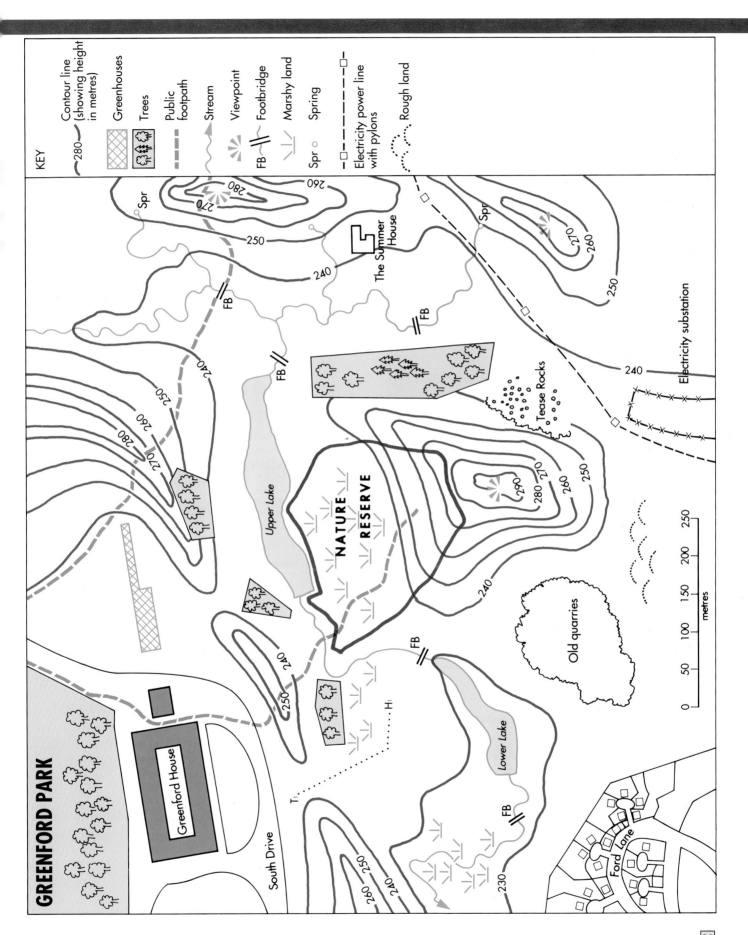

GREENFORD PARK

Greenford House

South Drive

Upper Lake

NATURE RESERVE

The Summer House

Tease Rocks

Old quarries

Lower Lake

Ford Lane

Electricity substation

Spr

FB

KEY

280	Contour line (showing height in metres)
	Greenhouses
	Trees
	Public footpath
	Stream
	Viewpoint
FB	Footbridge
	Marshy land
Spr ○	Spring
	Electricity power line with pylons
	Rough land

0 50 100 150 200 250
metres

Monitoring pollution
Satellite images

A space satellite in orbit.

Iraq pumps oil into the sea to hinder landing

The Gulf is being flooded with Kuwaiti oil. Experts estimate that a million birds could die. What hope is there for the Gulf after the war ends?

Catastrophe!

Kuwait 'could burn for a year'

The first space satellite was launched by the former USSR in 1957. It was called Sputnik 1 and as it circled in orbit, it relayed a signal back to the Earth. Soon technology advanced so that photographs of the Earth could be taken from space satellites and relayed back to the Earth. Such photographs are called *satellite images.*

Satellite images are sometimes black-and-white photographs, such as the images of cloud patterns used in weather forecasting. Other images are colour photographs of the Earth. Yet other images are not really photographs at all. These are *false-colour images* showing different kinds of patterns.

There are many uses of satellite images, including the search for resources (such as oil or water) and military uses. For some purposes, false-colour *infrared images* are required. By picking out surface temperature, these show clearly features at ground level, even when the surface is shrouded in cloud or mist.

You are an environmental consultant, hired by the United Nations to monitor pollution in the Persian Gulf. The satellite images opposite indicate a growing problem of oil pollution in this area.

Prepare a report on the oil pollution situation. You will need to include sketch maps showing the extent of the oil pollution in the Persian Gulf on each day for which you have information. Also, you must work out the rate at which the oil slick is spreading and the overall direction of its spread. Finally, produce a sketch map to show the area you expect will be affected by oil pollution in the Persian Gulf after a further 10 days have passed. An atlas map of the area will be useful for this task.

24TH JANUARY 1991

OIL
SLICK

1ST FEBRUARY 1991

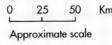

0   25   50   Km

Approximate scale

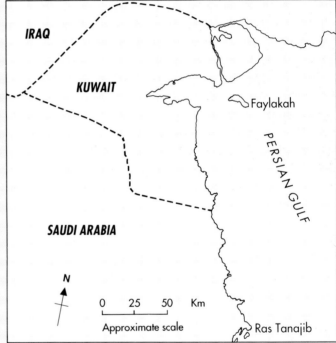

IRAQ

KUWAIT

Faylakah

PERSIAN GULF

SAUDI ARABIA

N

0   25   50   Km

Approximate scale

Ras Tanajib

OIL
SLICK

Looking into the past
Thematic maps

If you took away all of the place names from the map opposite, you would have a *dot map*. This is a type of *thematic map* (a map which shows one particular feature of the geography of an area).

The villages and towns marked on the map are very old. They date back about 1,500 years and were set up by the Danes and Anglo-Saxons – peoples who invaded Britain from Europe. The names of these earliest primary settlements have these endings:

borough   bury   ing

ham   ton

tone   by

toft   ford   hoe

worth   don

In time, technology improved and by about a thousand years ago, these people were able to clear thick woodland, plough wetter land and drain marshes so as to create newer secondary settlements. These have the following place-name endings:

-hall

-grave

-cote

-halse   -ley

-cot

-field   -thorp

-more

-dene

-den

In the area shown on the map opposite, setting up these secondary settlements involved clearing a forest that covered much of the region.

As County Historian for the map area, use the map evidence to create two dot maps to show:

a the pattern of primary settlements, and

b the pattern of secondary settlements.

Try to describe and explain the differences between the two dot maps.

When you have finished, draw a sketch map to show the area that would probably have been covered by forest in the region a thousand years ago (before the secondary settlements came along).

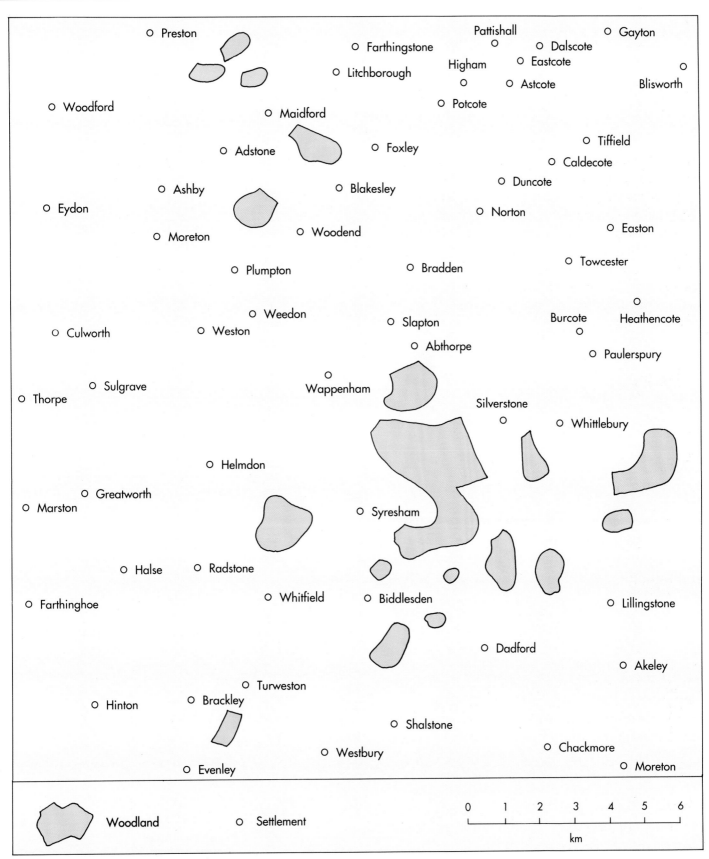

Settlements in south Northamptonshire.

Parcel delivery
Reference and location

The use of 4-figure coordinates to pinpoint places on a map was introduced on page 6. However, this method of describing points on a map can only pinpoint places where eastings and northings intersect. To pinpoint *any* place on a map, some other method is needed.

The Royal Mail uses a system of *postcodes*, which pins down letter deliveries to small map areas. For example:

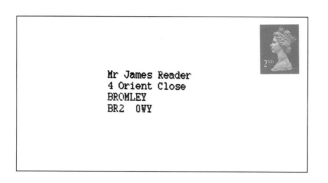

BR2 0WY is a postcode in Bromley (a district near London). BR stands for Bromley, and the other letters and numbers pinpoint the location of the address to an area containing no more than 15 letterboxes.

To describe precise map locations, the usual method used is a *6-figure grid reference*. For example, the youth hostel in King's Lynn, shown on this diagram, is at GR 616199. The first two numbers of the reference are for the easting to the left of the youth hostel (61). The third number shows how many tenths of the way towards the next easting the youth hostel is located (6 tenths). The next two numbers are for the northing directly below it (19). The final number shows how many tenths of the way towards the next northing it is located (9 tenths). There is a church with a spire located exactly on northing 19. Its 6-figure grid reference is 626190.

You work for a parcel delivery service called 'Nextnight', serving the King's Lynn area. As this is a private delivery service you can't use the Royal Mail postcode system to record address locations on your computerised sorting machine. Nextnight require you to reference each customer in the area using 6-figure grid references.

▷ What references will you type into the computer for each of the following customers?

King's Lynn Railway Station	Rising Lodge
Castle Rising Hospital	King's Lynn Town Hall
Sugar Factory	King's Lynn Hospital
North Wootton Inn	Warren Farm
North Runcton Church	The Elms Nurseries
King's Lynn Bus Station	Mintlyn Farm

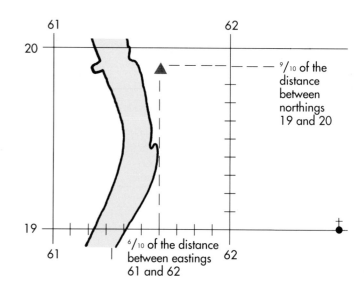

Rock around the clock
Reference and longitude

On a world scale, lines of latitude and longitude are used to describe the location of places. *Lines of longitude* circle the Earth from the North Pole to the South Pole. Starting from the 0 degrees line of longitude (which runs through Greenwich in London), longitude is measured in degrees east or west of Greenwich. *Lines of latitude* circle the Earth at right-angles (90 degrees) to the lines of longitude. Important lines of latitude are the Equator and the two Tropics of Capricorn and Cancer.

Time differences can also be calculated using longitude. There is a four-minute difference in time for each degree of longitude (although in reality, within countries, people use 'standard' time zones).

The simple rule is that places to the west of us are behind us in time. Places to the east of us are ahead of us in time.

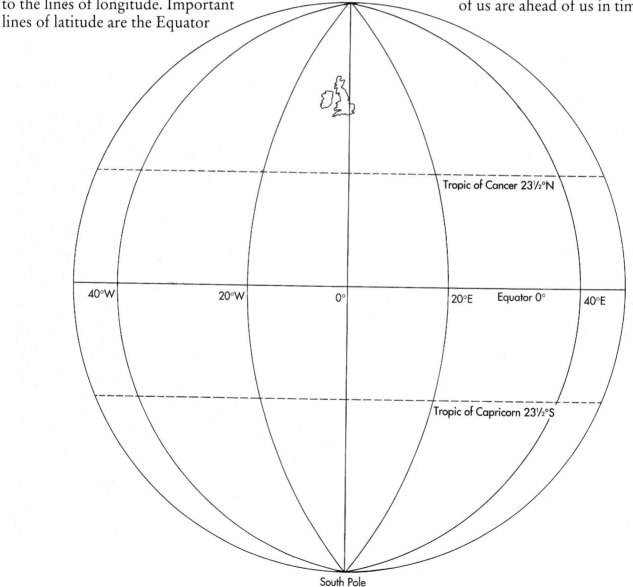

North Pole

Tropic of Cancer 23½°N

40°W   20°W   0°   20°E   Equator 0°   40°E

Tropic of Capricorn 23½°S

South Pole

You are the lead singer of the 'Time Zones', the world's most popular rock group. You are due to appear in concert in Central Park, New York at 11 pm (local time) on 12th August, topping the bill at a huge charity event.

There is only one problem: you are notorious for failing to be on time for concerts. Will you make it in time?

You set off by aeroplane from Heathrow Airport (London) at 5.00 am on 11th August, the day before your New York concert date. First though you have to visit other parts of the world. A friend has been injured in Austria, and you are anxious to see her in Vienna. The flight to Vienna takes 3 hours. You have 4 hours there before you must fly to Brazil. The flight to Belo Horizonte takes 12 hours and you spend 3 hours there making your TV appearance before jetting off for a brief concert performance in Johannesburg in South Africa. The flight to Johannesburg takes 10 hours. You have just 3 hours there, then fly on to New York. That flight takes 12 hours.

▷ At what time will you arrive in New York? Will you be in time for the concert?

Use an atlas to help you solve this problem. The atlas will contain information you need about the longitude of the places described here.

A rock concert in Central Park, New York.

Using isopleths
Thematic maps

Another type of thematic map used in geography is the isopleth map. An *isopleth* is a line that joins up places which are equal for some measure. For example, it could be air pressure (*isobars*), temperature (*isotherms*) or travel time (*isotims*).

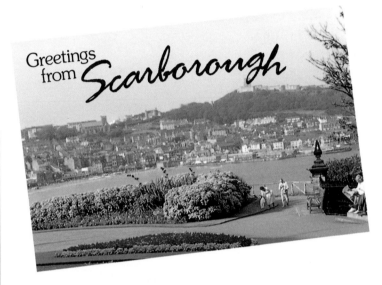
Greetings from *Scarborough*

Are you planning a holiday? Where would be the best place to go in terms of weather for your holiday in Britain?

Using the isopleth maps opposite, complete a copy of the table shown below. You will need to fill in the figures for the weather conditions at the resorts, using the isopleth maps. Where the resort lies in between two lines, you will need to estimate the figure. Then rank the resorts from 1 (best) to 10 (worst) for each of the three weather features shown on the maps.

Finally, add up the ranks across the columns. The lowest total score is the best resort in terms of weather. However, you should remember there are lots of other factors a holidaymaker would need to take into account when choosing a holiday destination.

When you have completed the table, make a poster for the best resort's tourist board, explaining its advantages as a resort.

The information at the bottom of page 33 is about two Mediterranean resorts. What sort of advantages do they seem to have over our British resorts?

Resort	July temperature & rank		Rain days & rank		Sunshine hours & rank		Total rank
Blackpool (B)							
Rhyl (R)							
Aberystwyth (A)							
Minehead (Mi)							
Newquay (N)							
Torquay (T)							
Bournemouth (Bo)							
Margate (M)							
Cromer (C)							
Scarborough (S)							
Portrush (P)							

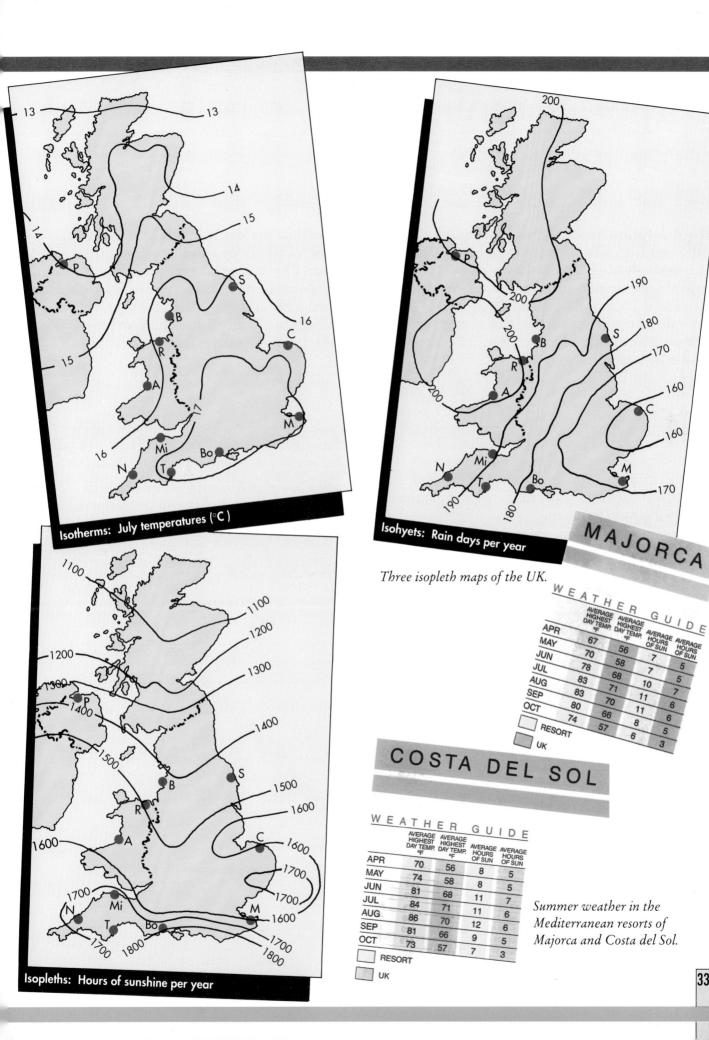

Isotherms: July temperatures (°C)

Isohyets: Rain days per year

Isopleths: Hours of sunshine per year

Three isopleth maps of the UK.

MAJORCA

WEATHER GUIDE

	AVERAGE HIGHEST DAY TEMP. °F	AVERAGE HIGHEST DAY TEMP. °F	AVERAGE HOURS OF SUN	AVERAGE HOURS OF SUN
APR	67	56	7	5
MAY	70	58	7	5
JUN	78	68	10	5
JUL	83	71	11	7
AUG	83	70	11	6
SEP	80	66	8	5
OCT	74	57	6	3

☐ RESORT
▦ UK

COSTA DEL SOL

WEATHER GUIDE

	AVERAGE HIGHEST DAY TEMP. °F	AVERAGE HIGHEST DAY TEMP. °F	AVERAGE HOURS OF SUN	AVERAGE HOURS OF SUN
APR	70	56	8	5
MAY	74	58	8	5
JUN	81	68	11	7
JUL	84	71	11	6
AUG	86	70	12	6
SEP	81	66	9	5
OCT	73	57	7	3

☐ RESORT
▦ UK

Summer weather in the Mediterranean resorts of Majorca and Costa del Sol.

Airport planning
Location decisions

When decisions have to be made about what to build and where, maps are of great use to the people involved in making the decisions.

Town and country planners are very much involved in such problems and decisions, for example where a bypass should be routed, where new homes should be built, or where a factory should be located.

From time to time, planners have looked at possible locations for building a new airport in southern England, to take the pressure off existing airports near London at Heathrow, Gatwick and Stansted. One area considered for a possible new site is between Bedford and Northampton (the area shown in the map extract opposite).

You are an airport planner, asked to consider this area as a possible new airport location. You are required to produce a plan (in the form of a sketch map) showing the following features:

1 *The position of the main runway for a new airport* This should be about 4 kilometres long. You will need to consider its location very carefully. As with airports generally, a flat site is very important. Crosswinds can also be a problem at airports, so you will need to consider local wind conditions as shown in the rose diagram on the right.

2 *Noise impact corridor* This will be an area badly affected by noise pollution extending 2 kilometres on either side of the runway and up to 4 kilometres beyond each end of the runway. This corridor should be clearly marked on your plan and shaded. Mark on any settlements that are located within or near to this corridor.

3 *Airport terminal buildings* These will occupy an area equivalent to 1 square kilometre.

4 *Access roads* These should link with any existing major roads in the area.

5 *Re-alignment of any electricity lines or radio masts in the low-flying vicinity of the airport.*

When your plan is complete, write a brief report, summing up what you see as the main advantages and disadvantages of this area as a possible site for a new airport.

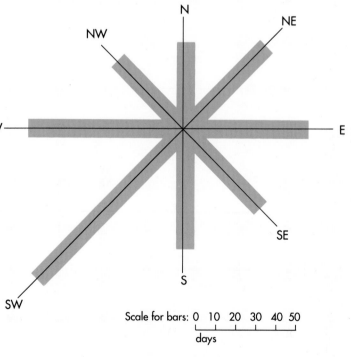

Wind rose for the new airport location.

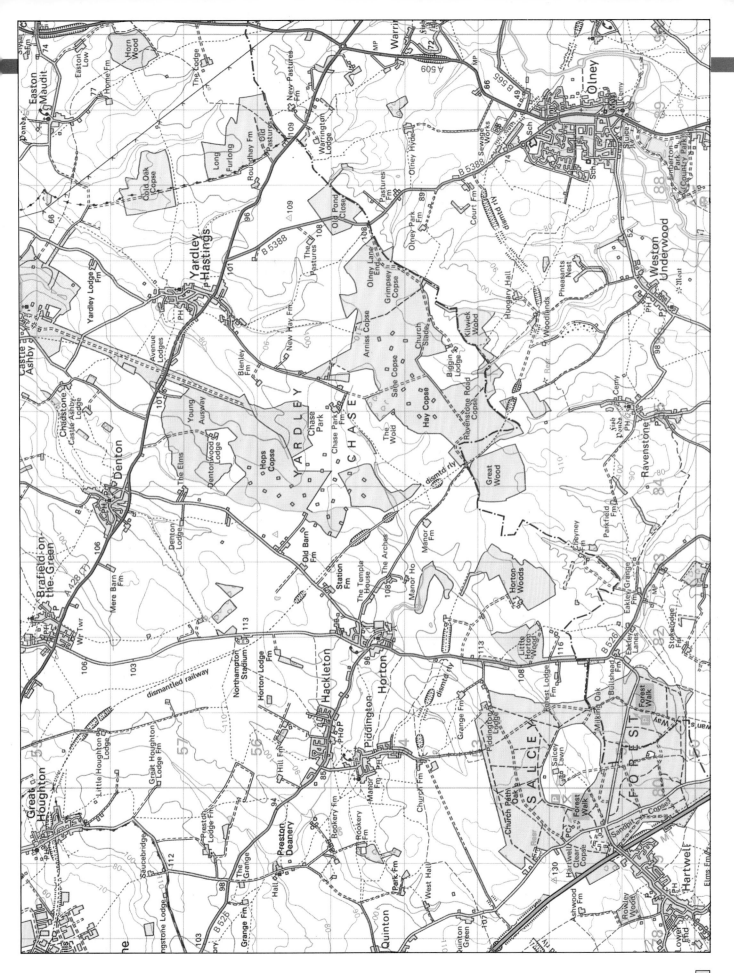

Solving a crime
Map symbols and shadings

You are an officer in the Serious Crime Squad. The heiress to a millionaire's fortune has been kidnapped, and you must try to establish where she is being held. The only items of evidence you have to go on are the contents of her handbag, which was left in a lay-by some distance away from where she was kidnapped. These are shown below and include five photographs that were on a film in her camera. They show places she visited on a walking holiday in the Fell District National Park immediately prior to her kidnap.

Work out the route that you think she followed through the area. You may find it helpful to refer to the map symbols shown on page 48. Then decide where you think the heiress may be held.

When your investigation is complete, prepare a brief report presenting your conclusions. This should include a sketch map showing the route you think the woman followed whilst visiting the area.

'The evidence.'

Part of the Fell District National Park.

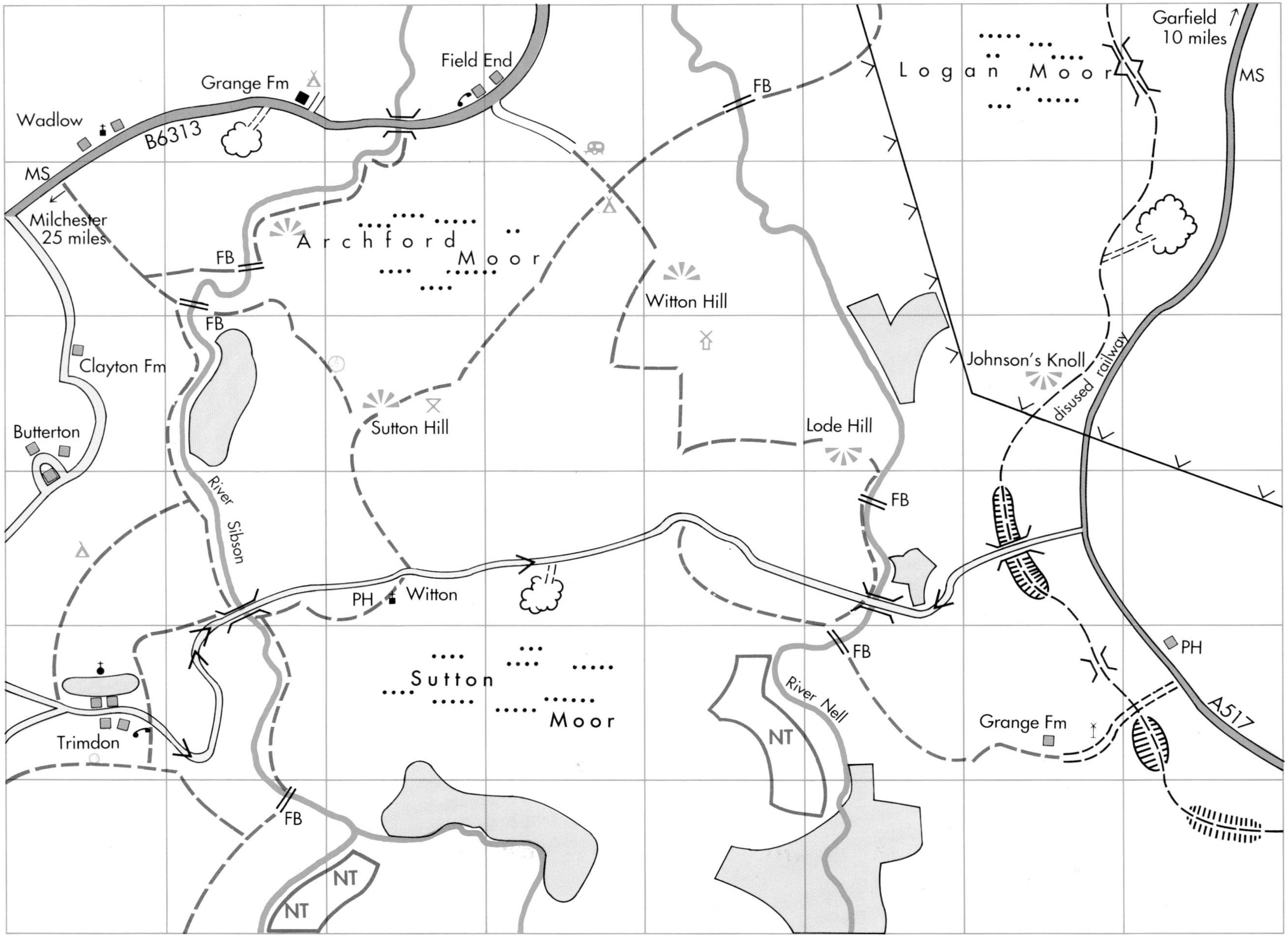

Garfield ↑
10 miles

MS

A517

PH

L o g a n   M o o r

disused railway

Johnson's Knoll

Grange Fm

FB

Lode Hill

FB

FB

River Nell

NT

FB

Witton Hill

Field End

A r c h f o r d   M o o r

Sutton Hill

S u t t o n   M o o r

NT

NT

Grange Fm

Wadlow

B6313

MS

Milchester
25 miles

Clayton Fm

FB

FB

River   Sibson

Witton

PH

FB

Butterton

Trimdon

Locating a factory
Location decisions and relief

Contour information on maps allows you to calculate how far you can see from a particular viewpoint. This is called *inter-visibility*. For example, in the sketch map on the right it would be possible to see the windmill from point A, but not the club house or youth hostel.

A good idea of inter-visibility can be gained from laying the edge of a piece of paper between two points and marking and numbering the contours lying between them.

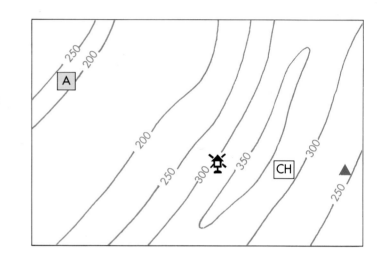

You are a planning consultant and have been approached by United Meat Products Ltd to advise on a suitable location for their new factory in the area shown on the map opposite.

You are asked to produce a simple sketch map showing the suggested location, and a brief written report justifying your choice. You must bear in mind the following:

1 Because of the size of the factory, the firm wants to find a fairly secluded location.

2 The factory will include a 50-metre high chimney, putting some unpleasant waste gases and smells into the air. You will need to try to find a location where views of the chimney from the surrounding area will be kept to a minimum. It is estimated that the wind will blow the fumes up to 4 kilometres downwind before they are dispersed in the air. Therefore you should consider the information in the wind rose shown here in making your decision.

3 Good access to road transport is important.

4 It will be helpful if the factory is not too far away from a larger settlement from which labour can be drawn.

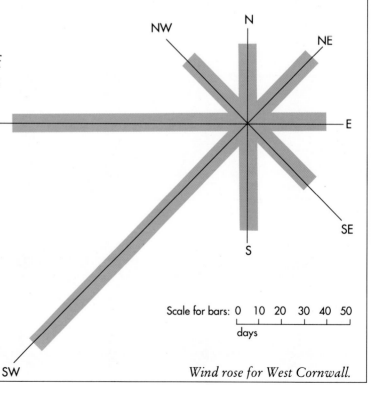

Scale for bars: 0 10 20 30 40 50
days

Wind rose for West Cornwall.

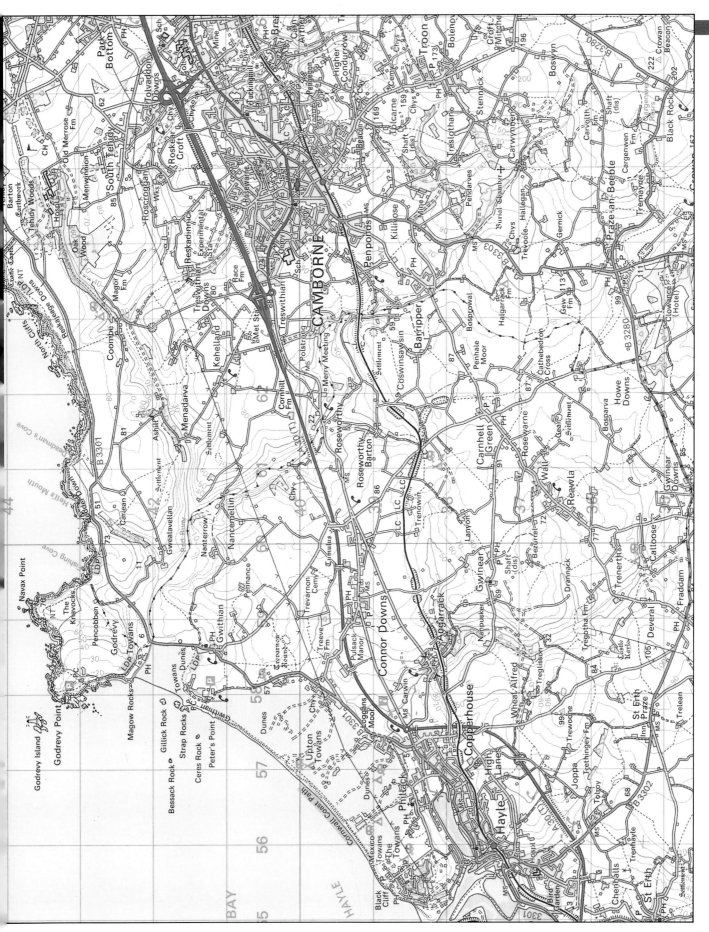

Search and rescue
Synoptic charts

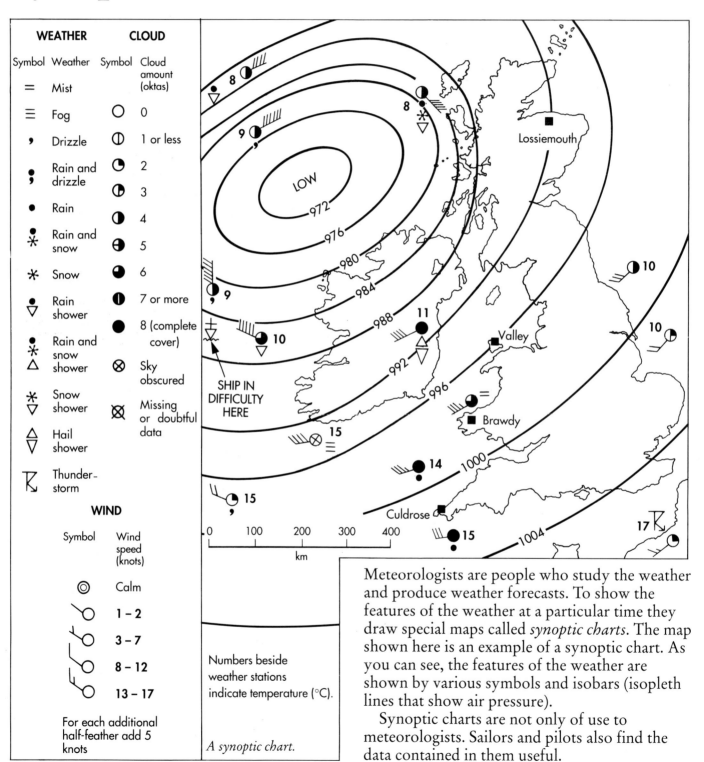

WEATHER

Symbol	Weather
=	Mist
≡	Fog
,	Drizzle
,̣	Rain and drizzle
•	Rain
*	Rain and snow
＊	Snow
•̽	Rain shower
•＊△	Rain and snow shower
＊̽	Snow shower
△̽	Hail shower
⚡	Thunder-storm

CLOUD

Symbol	Cloud amount (oktas)
○	0
◑	1 or less
◕	2
◑	3
◐	4
◕	5
◑	6
◑	7 or more
●	8 (complete cover)
⊗	Sky obscured
⊠	Missing or doubtful data

WIND

Symbol	Wind speed (knots)
◎	Calm
	1 – 2
	3 – 7
	8 – 12
	13 – 17

For each additional half-feather add 5 knots

Numbers beside weather stations indicate temperature (°C).

A synoptic chart.

Meteorologists are people who study the weather and produce weather forecasts. To show the features of the weather at a particular time they draw special maps called *synoptic charts*. The map shown here is an example of a synoptic chart. As you can see, the features of the weather are shown by various symbols and isobars (isopleth lines that show air pressure).

Synoptic charts are not only of use to meteorologists. Sailors and pilots also find the data contained in them useful.

You are the assistant co-ordinator of RAF search and rescue services for the UK. You have four search and rescue bases where Sea King helicopters are stationed. They are at Culdrose, Brawdy, Valley and Lossiemouth. A 'Mayday' distress signal has been received from a ship in difficulty in the Atlantic Ocean to the west of Ireland.

You have an important decision to make in a short time:

▷ From which of the four search and rescue stations should you send a helicopter?

To help you make this decision, you have an up-to-the-minute synoptic chart showing weather conditions in the area (see opposite).

In particular, you will need to consider from which base a helicopter will be able to arrive quickest. If the ship's crew members are injured, return time to base will also be an important consideration.

Distance from the base to the ship is not the only factor to consider. A helicopter flying into the wind has its maximum speed reduced, while one flying with the wind has its maximum speed increased. This effect is shown in the graph below. Flying with a crosswind, a helicopter maintains normal maximum speed, which is 150 kilometres per hour.

In deciding where to send a helicopter from, you will need to calculate the return journey time from the ship to each base.

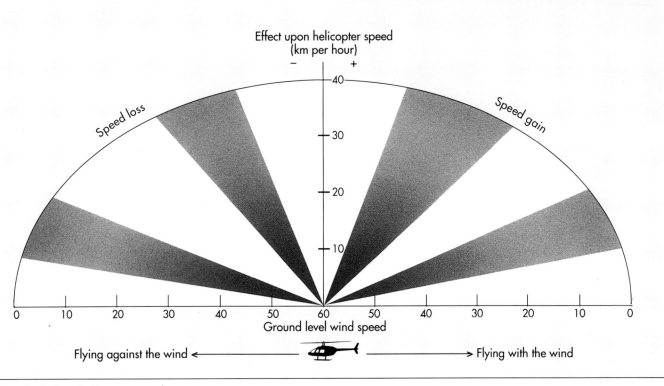

Effect of wind on helicopter speed.

Map and compass
Making connections

Orienteering is a popular sport throughout Europe. Basically it involves running through woodland or over rough land in order to reach several checkpoints. The orienteer is free to select the route he or she feels is the best. Special maps like the one opposite are used in orienteering. They give a detailed picture of the terrain to be covered, including information about any obstacles such as steep slopes or thick vegetation that may need to be avoided.

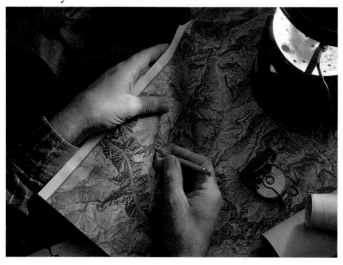

If you were orienteering the Bryn-engan course shown on the map, what route would you follow? Between the start and the finish you must visit each of the checkpoints marked (+). Mark on a tracing overlay your chosen route. You should bear in mind the following:

1 A straight line is not always the best route to follow between two checkpoints; obstacles may need to be avoided along the way.

2 An orienteer can cover the ground much quicker along a road or track.

Using a compass or protractor, work out the bearing along which you would need to set off from the start and from each checkpoint.

Work out the total distance covered by your route. How long would it take you? (An orienteer can run 200 metres per minute along a track and 100 metres per minute over rough ground. In places such as on very steep slopes, only walking is possible, 50 metres being covered per minute.)

Compare your route, distance and time with other members of your class to see who has the best route.

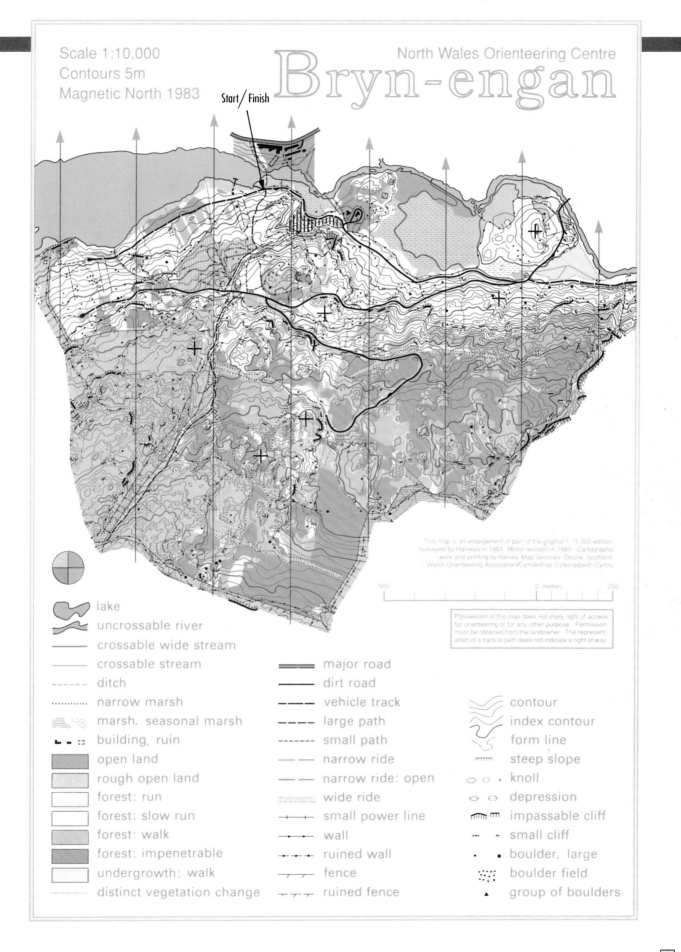

Scale 1:10,000
Contours 5m
Magnetic North 1983

North Wales Orienteering Centre
Bryn-engan

Start / Finish

This map is an enlargement of part of the original 1:15,000 edition, surveyed by Harveys in 1983. Minor revision in 1989. Cartographic work and printing by Harvey Map Services, Doune, Scotland. © Welsh Orienteering Association/Cymdeithas Cyfeiriadaeth Cymru

500   0 metres   250

lake
uncrossable river
crossable wide stream
crossable stream
ditch
narrow marsh
marsh, seasonal marsh
building, ruin
open land
rough open land
forest: run
forest: slow run
forest: walk
forest: impenetrable
undergrowth: walk
distinct vegetation change

major road
dirt road
vehicle track
large path
small path
narrow ride
narrow ride: open
wide ride
small power line
wall
ruined wall
fence
ruined fence

contour
index contour
form line
steep slope
knoll
depression
impassable cliff
small cliff
boulder, large
boulder field
group of boulders

A problem of movement
Flow maps

When movements of people or things are studied in geography, a special type of thematic map is used. This is called a *flow map*. Usually this shows the number on the move at different places on a map by arrows or lines of varying thickness. The example here shows the outward movement of goods from some of the UK's major ports.

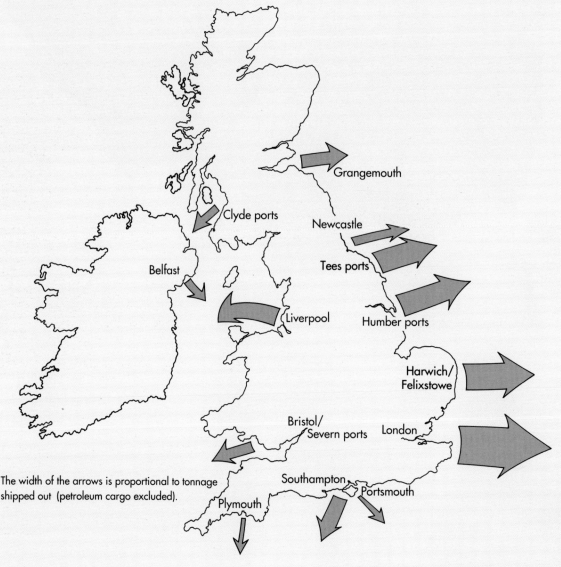

Grangemouth

Clyde ports

Newcastle

Belfast

Tees ports

Liverpool

Humber ports

Harwich/
Felixstowe

Bristol/
Severn ports

London

The width of the arrows is proportional to tonnage shipped out (petroleum cargo excluded).

Southampton

Portsmouth

Plymouth

Sea-borne trade leaving major UK ports, 1988.

You are the headteacher of St Elias School, which has a problem of movement along its corridors. You have recently received a number of complaints from parents about congestion in the school corridors. In response, you have asked the pupils to carry out a survey of the numbers moving in the corridors at different lesson changes. The results of this are shown on the plan of the school below.

The school governors have asked you to report on the problem and propose a solution to it at their next meeting. To do this you will need to construct a flow map using the information provided by the pupils' survey. Decide on a suitable scale for the thickness of the arrows. First you will need to work out the maximum flow in any area. You will also need to explain your proposed solution both in writing and with the aid of a sketch plan of the school.

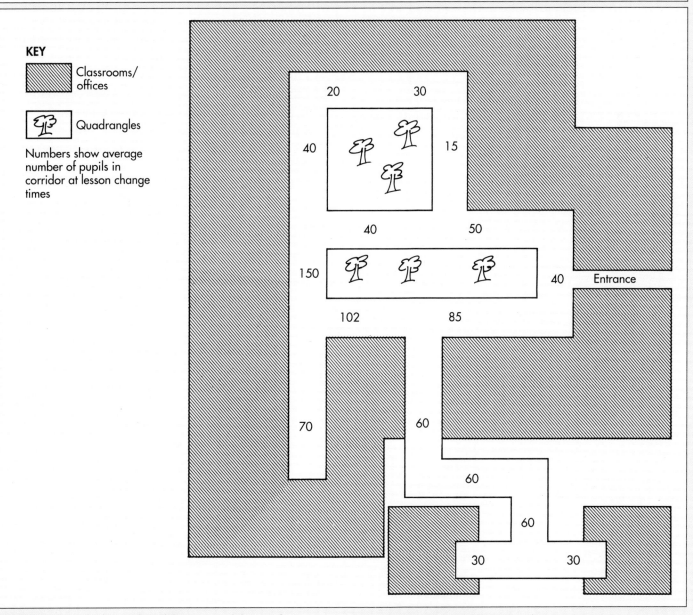

KEY

Classrooms/ offices

Quadrangles

Numbers show average number of pupils in corridor at lesson change times

20   30

40   15

40   50

150   40   Entrance

102   85

70   60

60

60

30   30

Perhaps your own school has a problem of movement that you could investigate.

Making plans
Thematic maps and location decisions

Some maps are designed to show future changes that are in store for an area. These are another form of thematic map and are called *plans*.

In the UK, town and country planners produce various plans which show how they intend to direct the future use and development of land. A district plan covers the planned future use and development of your local area, and copies of this are available from local council offices.

Producing a plan requires much skill, with careful consideration given to deciding what should be allowed to develop where.

Extract from a district plan.

You are a planning expert. You have been asked to produce a plan for a new village to be built near to a motorway junction in the south of England. The base map of the area is shown opposite. Note the dimensions of the area as indicated by the scale.

The new village will contain various buildings (drawn to scale and shown opposite). You will also be allowed to plant trees and include some new local roads. You will need to think very carefully about where buildings will be best placed.

In creating your plan you must try to achieve the following major objectives:

– A neighbourhood that will be pleasant and convenient to live in.
– Keep apart land uses that do not go together. For example, try to keep busy traffic out of housing areas.

Decide for yourself a third major objective. When your plan is complete, write a brief report describing and explaining its main features.

LOCAL PLAN
PROPOSALS MAP No 1
ENVIRONMENT ZONES

- Special Landscape Area, ENV
- Local Landscape Area, ENV2
- Class XIV Area of Restriction, HI5
- Green Barrier, ENV3
- Conservation Area, ENV18, 19

SITE SPECIFIC POLICIES

- Housing, H4, 5, 8, 15
- Shopping, S1, S16
- Tourism, T2, 7, 8
- Economic Development, E4, 5, 6, 10, 12
- Recreation & Community Facilities RC 222, 5, 7, 8
- Transport, TR1, 2

BOUNDARIES

- Boundary of Local Plan
- Boundary of Urban Area
- Rural Settlement

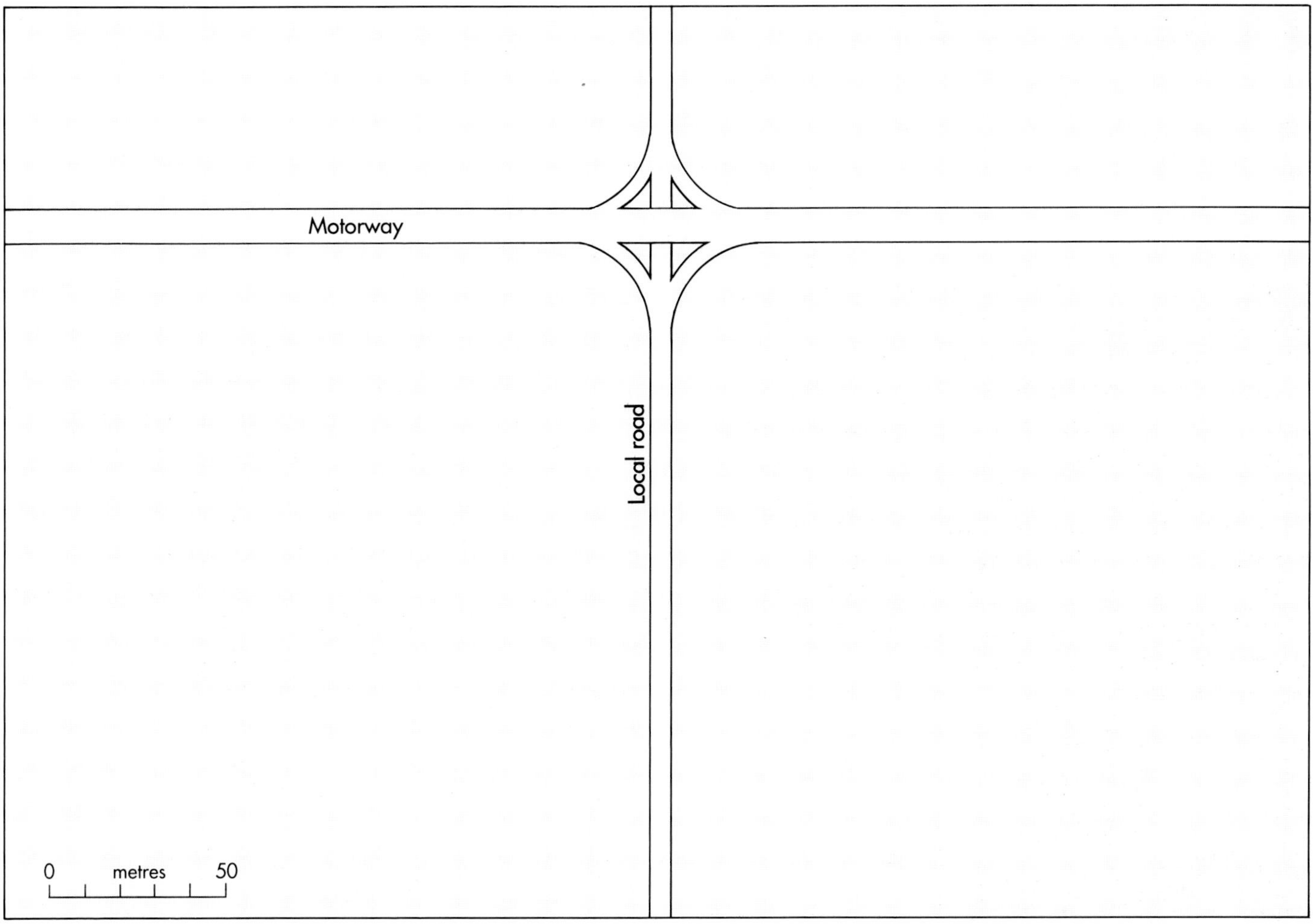

Motorway

Local road

0 metres 50

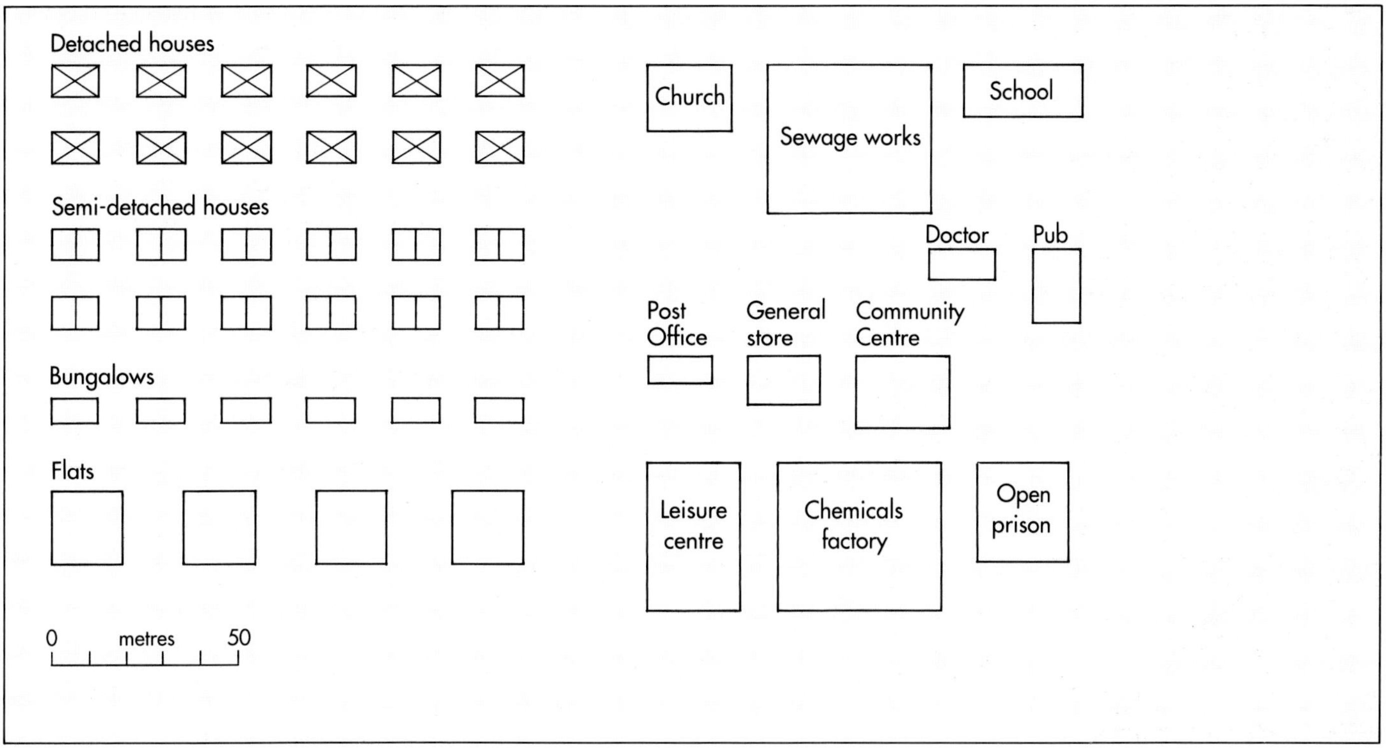

Detached houses

Semi-detached houses

Bungalows

Flats

0 metres 50

Church

Sewage works

School

Doctor

Pub

Post Office

General store

Community Centre

Leisure centre

Chemicals factory

Open prison

Base map for a new village plan.

Ordnance Survey
1 : 50 000 map symbols

ROADS AND PATHS

Service area M1
Elevated
Motorway (dual carriageway)

Junction number 1

Dual carriageway
Main road

Secondary road

Bridge

Road generally less than 4 m wide

Other road, drive or track

Gradient: 1 in 5 and steeper
1 in 7 to 1 in 5

Footpath

TOURIST INFORMATION

Information centre

Caravan site

Picnic site

Youth hostel

Viewpoint

Telephone, public/motoring
organisation

Camp site

RAILWAYS

Track multiple or single

a   b
Station (a) principal
(b) closed to passengers

Embankment

Cutting

WATER FEATURES

Cliff
High water mark
Slopes
Low water mark
Marsh or salting
Towpath   Lock
Flat rock
Lighthouse (in use)
Aqueduct
Weir
Ford
Sand
Beacon
Bridge
Normal tidal limit
Lighthouse (disused)
Footbridge
Dunes
Shingle
Mud
Canal (dry)

GENERAL FEATURES

Mixed wood
Glasshouse

Park or ornamental grounds
Triangulation pillar

Windmill with or without sails

Bracken, heath and
rough grassland
Windpump

Broadcasting station
(mast or tower)

Church
or
Chapel

with tower
Electricity transmission line

with spire
County, Region
or Islands Area

without tower or spire
NT
National Trust

ABBREVIATIONS

P   Post office
PH   Public house
MS   Milestone
MP   Milepost
CH   Clubhouse